YOUNG EINSTEIN

DISCOVERING NATURE

Welcome to our *Young Einstein* series of educational resource books, a series specifically designed to give young minds the tools they need to embrace and explore the mysteries and miracles of the world around them.

Each books is complete with clear text introducing the scientific principles, examples of those concepts at work, a step-by-step guide to explore each new concept, and further questions and ideas to urge young scientists on to more exploring.

The *Young Einstein* series is designed with any classroom in mind, aiding teachers and students both in the school environment and the at-home classroom by both educating children about the amazing world in which they live, and more importantly, giving young scientists the tools they need to explore and learn about their world on their own.

While having an adult's help is always important with the set-up and execution of experiments, each project in these books is specifically designed to place the ability to discover in the hands of young scientists. The pictures of each part of the experiments and interactive glossary are invaluable tools to aid young learners in their quest of understanding.

We are sure your young scientists will finish these books with a new understanding of the world around them, and newfound abilities to explore and discover their world on their own.

"Imagination is more important than knowledge. For knowledge is limited to all we now know and understand, while imagination embraces the entire world, and all there ever will be to know and understand." - Albert Einstein

© 2012 Flowerpot Press

Flowerpot Press
142 2nd Avenue North
Franklin, TN 37064

Flowerpot Press is a division of Kamalu, LLC,
Franklin, TN, U.S.A.,
and Mitso Media, Inc., Oakville, ON, Canada.

ISBN 978-1-77093-601-0

Illustrator: Tony Kenyon

Printed in China.

All Year Round

Sally Hewitt

FLOWERPOT PRESS

Nashville • Toronto

Contents

Introduction

As the seasons change, you will see many differences in the plants and animals around you. Have fun keeping a nature diary, listen for the changing sounds throughout the year, and keep a lookout for migrating birds. Paint sunflower pots, make pictures from autumn leaves, and learn how you can help keep animals warm in the winter.

Hints and Tips

- Do not pick leaves or flowers from a plant. Only take ones that are already on the ground.

Try to look at creatures without disturbing them. If you do move them, always return them to the place where you found them.

Before touching soil or plants, cover any cuts with an adhesive bandage.

Do not rub your face or eyes when working with plants or soil. Always wash your hands afterwards.

Nature Diary

Look and listen carefully, and you will notice fascinating things happening in nature all year round. You can make a nature diary to keep a record of the things you spot at different times of year, both in the city and the countryside.

Pheasant

Scot's pine

Month by Month

1 To make a nature diary, you will need a large pad, pen and pencils, glue, and tape. Make a page for each month, like the one in the picture.

2 Collect leaves and pine needles from the ground, let them dry, then glue them into your diary. Make sure you label them.

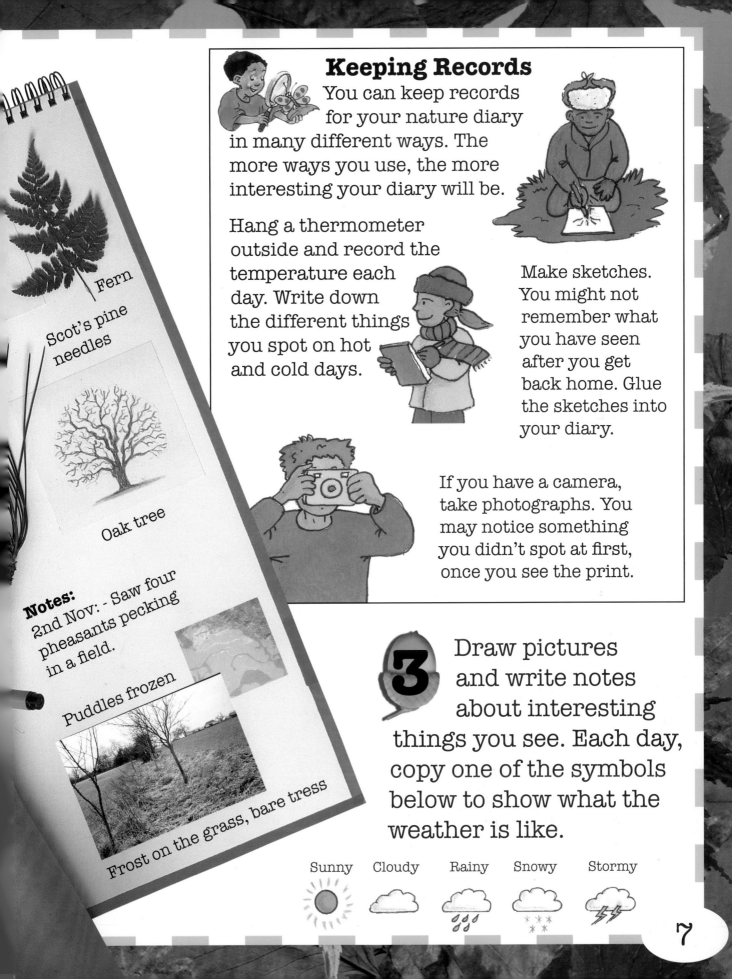

Keeping Records

You can keep records for your nature diary in many different ways. The more ways you use, the more interesting your diary will be.

Hang a thermometer outside and record the temperature each day. Write down the different things you spot on hot and cold days.

Make sketches. You might not remember what you have seen after you get back home. Glue the sketches into your diary.

If you have a camera, take photographs. You may notice something you didn't spot at first, once you see the print.

Fern

Scot's pine needles

Oak tree

Notes:
2nd Nov: - Saw four pheasants pecking in a field.

Puddles frozen

Frost on the grass, bare tress

3 Draw pictures and write notes about interesting things you see. Each day, copy one of the symbols below to show what the weather is like.

Sunny   Cloudy   Rainy   Snowy   Stormy

7

Seasons

As spring turns to summer, then to fall, and winter, the weather and the world around you changes. Look out for changes in the landscape and in plants and animals during each season of the year.

Changing Places

1 Choose a place that is easy for you to visit often. (Try to find somewhere with a tree, plants, and maybe a pond.)

2 In each season, paint a picture or take a photograph of the place you have chosen. If you paint, be sure to copy the colors carefully.

3 Glue your pictures onto colored cardstock or construction paper and label them with the season. Spot the differences between your pictures.

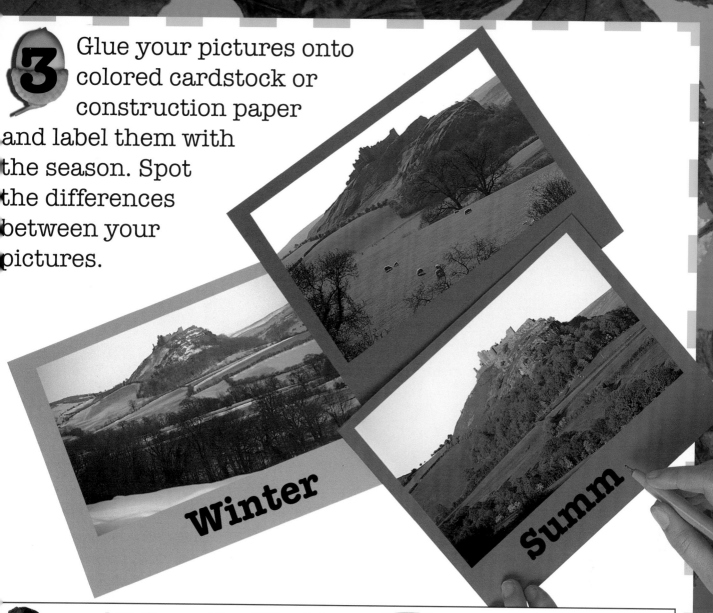

Winter

Summ

All Over the World

Each part of the world has its own kind of weather. Hot, dry places have different plants and animals than icy, cold places.

It is freezing all year round at the poles. Few plants grow, and animals have thick coats and an extra layer of fat.

Tropical rainforests are warm and wet all year. Plants grow thick and fast, and the forest teems with insects, birds, and other animals.

Deserts have little rain, so few plants grow there. When rain does fall, flowers burst from the ground in a carpet of color.

Window Box

You can grow plants all year round, even if you don't have a garden. Try planting herbs in a window box. Once they have grown, pinch the leaves to smell the herbs' fragrance.

Indoors and Outdoors

1 You will need packets of herb seeds and a window box with compost in it.

2 Sprinkle the seeds on the compost. Leave space between the different seeds. Lay more compost on top. Put the box on an indoor windowsill or, in spring or summer, outside.

4 When the herbs have grown, snip off the leaves to use for cooking. Only cut off what you need. The leaves will grow back again.

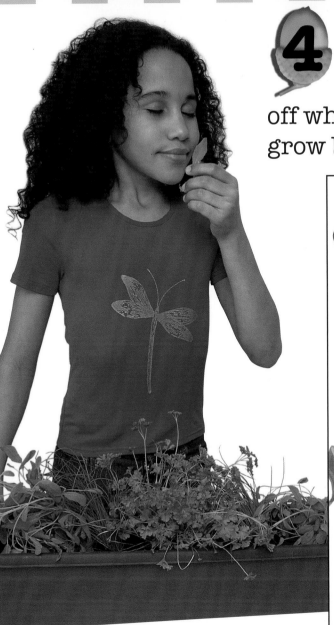

Herb Garden

Herbs from an herb garden can be used for flavoring food, brewing herbal teas, and treating illnesses.

Rosemary tea is good for soothing headaches and upset stomachs.

The leaves of chives give an onion flavor to salads.

Parsley stalks have a stronger flavor than the leaves.

Basil, when planted among other plants, helps keep insects away. You can also add its leaves to tomato dishes for a delicious flavor.

3 Water the herbs regularly. If they are outside, check that there has been enough rain.

Seasonal Sounds

Go outside and listen carefully. Some sounds you hear are made by people or machines, but others are noises made by nature. Make a note of all the natural sounds you can hear during different times of the year.

Nightingale

Listen Closely

1 In the early spring, listen for male birds singing to attract a mate. Later, baby birds cheep noisily for food.

Jay

2 In the summer, insects buzz among the flowers, and grasshoppers sing in the grass.

Fly

Grasshopper

Geese

3 In the fall, listen for wings beating as flocks of geese ~~fly~~ south for the winter. ~~In~~ the woods, listen for ~~n~~uts falling on crunchy ~~l~~eaves.

Chestnut

~~r~~ough ridges on the grasshopper's ~~b~~ack legs rub against its wings ~~to~~ make a chirping noise.

Croaking Frogs

In the spring, male frogs gather together in ponds and croak loudly. Each one is trying to attract a female to be their mate. They can even croak underwater.

Frog

Air sac

When a frog croaks, a pouch of skin under its chin fills with air and helps the croaking sound to carry over a distance. Some frogs are named after the sounds they make, such as the snoring puddle frog, which is found in parts of Africa.

4 In winter, listen for the harsh caw of crows and rooks. They nest in the tops of trees, and you can sometimes see them looking for food near trashcans or dumps.

Rook

Sunflowers

Sunflowers are very useful plants. Animals eat the leaves, yellow dye is made from the petals, and oil is pressed from the seeds. Plant a sunflower seed in spring, and by the summer it will have grown even taller than you!

Painting and Planting

1 Gather a packet of sunflower seeds, soil, three big flowerpots, and some paint.

2 Paint pictures of sunflowers on the outside of the pots. Plant two or three seeds in each pot. Water them regularly.

3 As the shoots appear, leave the strongest shoot in each pot to grow. Pull up the other ones.

4 Your sunflowers will grow very tall. You can support the stems with garden canes.

Follow the Sun

Although sunflowers do look like bright yellow suns, they are called "sunflowers" for a different reason. In the morning, they face the rising sun. As the sun moves throughout the day, the sunflowers turn their heads to follow the sun across the sky.

Noon

Morning

Evening

5 After the petals die, leave the flower heads for the birds. They will eat the seeds that form in the middle of the sunflower.

Butterflies and Moths

Butterflies visit flowers in the daytime. Moths often feed at night. They use their long feeding tubes like drinking straws to suck sweet juice called "nectar" from the flowers. Look for butterflies and moths when the flowers they feed on are in bloom.

Butterfly Watching

1 Butterflies are attracted to purple flowers with a strong scent, like buddleia flowers. (Buddleia is also called "the butterfly bush.")

2 Make sketches of butterflies you see, and take notes. This will help you look them up later in a field guide.

3 Use binoculars to help you spot butterflies. This will let you see their markings more clearly and watch without disturbing them. You might even see some having a drink from a puddle.

Nectar Eaters

Most butterflies live only for a short time in the summer when the flowers are out. Other creatures that drink nectar, such as hummingbirds, make long journeys to find flowers in bloom all year round.

Honeysuckle smells most strongly at night to attract moths.

Butterflies curl their feeding tubes under their heads when the aren't using them.

Tiny Australian honey possums have long tongues to lick nectar from banksia flowers.

A hummingbird hovers in front of a flower while it sucks nectar with its long tongue.

17

Collections

Go for a walk at any time of year and you will find all kinds of interesting natural things. Make a collection for each season, or for places you visit, like the park or the beach.

Make a Mini-Museum

1 Find a cardboard box with a good-sized base. Cut down the sides to make a frame.

2 Line the box with colored paper. (This will be the background for your mini-museum.)

Get an adult to help you.

Cockle shell

Garden snail shell

Chestnut

Chestnut husk

Maple leaf

Cedar c

3 Arrange the objects you collect in the box, then carefully glue them down. Label each item clearly.

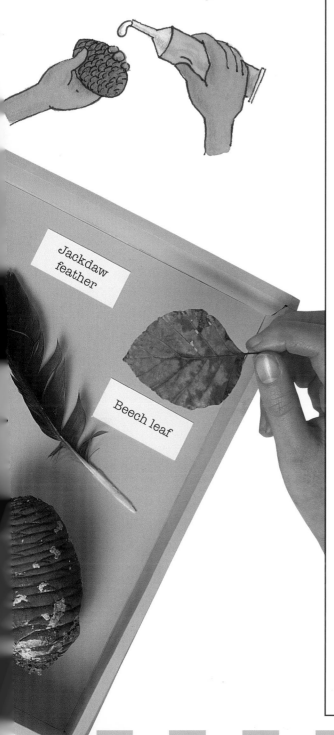

Jackdaw feather

Beech leaf

Flying Feathers

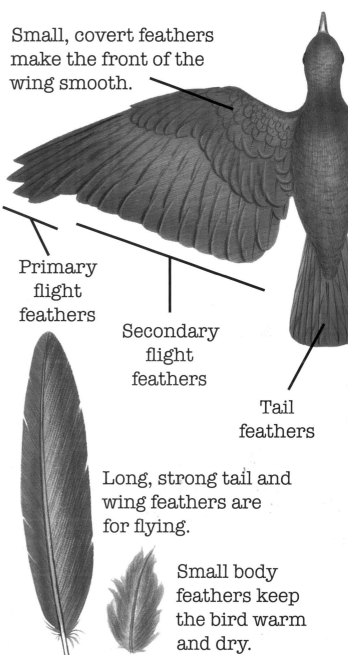

Birds are the only creatures that have feathers. Their feathers are shaped for the different jobs they have. You can tell which part of a bird's body a feather comes from just by looking at the feather.

Small, covert feathers make the front of the wing smooth.

Primary flight feathers

Secondary flight feathers

Tail feathers

Long, strong tail and wing feathers are for flying.

Small body feathers keep the bird warm and dry.

Fruit

Fruit is the part of a plant that holds the seeds for a new plant to grow. When a flower dies, a fruit grows in its place. Tiny apples start to grow after the apple blossoms die in the spring. By fall, the apples are ripe, juicy, and ready to eat.

Fruit Salad

1 Make a delicious fruit salad with lots of different fruits. First, cut each fruit into halves or quarters.

2 Scoop or pick out any seeds you can see. Look carefully at them through a magnifying glass. Remember which seeds come from which fruit.

Get an adult to help you.

Wild Berries

Wild berries are often bright and shiny. Birds spot them easily, and swoop down to eat them. The birds then scatter plant seeds in their droppings, letting new plants grow.

In winter, bright red holly berries make a feast for hungry birds when there is little food about.

Mistletoe grows on the branches of other trees. Its white berries are poisonous to people and animals.

In early fall, blackberries grow wild on prickly brambles. Birds, animals, and people like to eat them.

SOME BERRIES ARE POISONOUS. ALWAYS ASK AN ADULT.

3 Ask a friend to match each seed to the fruit it came from.

Changing Colors

Trees make food using the green color in their leaves, called "chlorophyll." In the summer, trees store the food they make. By fall, the chlorophyll is not needed. It breaks down and turns the leaves red, brown, gold, and orange.

Leaf Pictures

1 Collect as many different fall leaves as you can. Sort them into different shapes and colors.

2 You will need a clip frame and some colored paper. Cut out a piece of paper the same size as the clip frame, and lay it over the base of the frame.

Winter Leaves

By winter, most of the fallen leaves will have rotted away. Only leaf skeletons, evergreen leaves, and pine needles remain.

A leaf skeleton forms when the soft part of the leaf rots, leaving behind the tough stem and veins.

Holly trees are evergreens. They keep their shiny, prickly leaves all year round.

Pine needles are very thin leaves that can survive the cold. They stay on the trees all winter.

3 Arrange the leaves into a pattern or a picture, then lay the glass on top. The glass will hold the leaves in position.

Get an adult to help you.

Looking for Food

While in spring and summer animal and birds can usually find plenty of food to eat, many have to make long journeys to find enough food at other times of year. The journeys they make are called "migrations."

Spot Migrating Birds

1 You can often identify birds by the way they behave or fly. For example, before flying off, migrating swallows gather together on telephone wires.

2 Migrating geese fly off together in a "V" shape. Look out for geese and swallows in the fall. Make picture cards to keep a record of all the migrating birds you spot.

Finding the Way

Each year, animals, birds, and insects find their way across thousands of miles of land and sea. Whales swim halfway around the world, and caribou travel between the arctic plains and northern forests. Match the colored arrows to the arrows on the globe to see the migration routes.

➡ Humpback whales follow the coastline on their journey between cold polar and warm tropical seas.

➡ To find enough to eat, insect-eating birds, like swallows, fly south to spend the winter in Africa.

➡ Caribou follow the same paths each year. They go south in the fall and back north again in the spring.

➡ Arctic terns have a kind of built-in compass that helps them find their way from the North Pole to the South Pole, and back again.

➡ Monarch butterflies fly south from Canada in huge numbers to spend the winters in Mexico.

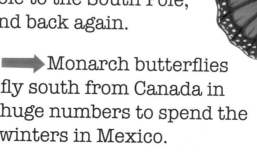

Hibernation

In the winter, when there is very little food around, bears, bats, hedgehogs, and dormice go into a long sleep called "hibernation." They hide away in a safe, dry place and sleep until the warm spring weather wakes them up again.

The Big Sleep

1 Make an animal shelter this fall. Collect dry sticks and some straw and leaves for warm bedding.

NEVER DISTURB A HIBERNATING ANIMAL.

2 In a quiet place outside, make a strong frame with the sticks. Cover it with dirt, grass, and leaves, and put the bedding inside.

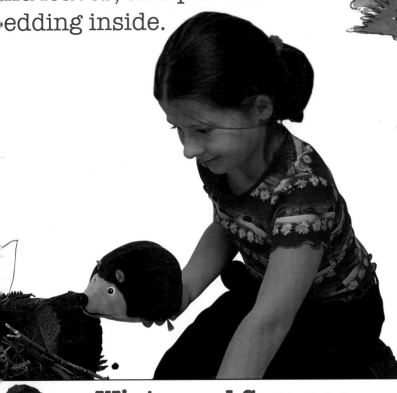

3 Put a soft toy inside to test how safe and dry it is. Don't disturb the shelter. Perhaps an animal will choose to hibernate there.

Winter and Summer

Some animals hibernate in winter. Some sleep in summer when water is scarce. This summer sleep is called "aestivation."

During the long winter sleep in her den, a mother bear wakes to give birth to her cubs.

During the winter, some kinds of bats hibernate together. They hang upside down in enormous groups in sheltered caves.

During the summer when their pools dry up, lungfish sleep in the mud. They use their lungs to breathe air.

Asleep in the Soil

Just as some animals curl up and sleep all winter, bulbs sleep too, buried in the soil. They wait for the warm spring weather to come before they start to grow. See how a hyacinth bulb will not grow in the dark, but starts to grow shoots in the light.

Grow a Bulb

1 Start this project in the fall. You will need a hyacinth bulb, a jar, and some toothpicks. Fill the jar nearly to the top with water.

2 Firmly stick four toothpicks around the middle of the bulb. Balance the bulb in the top of the jar so its base is in the water.

3 Put the bulb in a dark cupboard. Check it occasionally to make sure it has enough water.

4 Before winter is over, bring the bulb out into the light. It will start to grow, and you will soon have a beautifully scented hyacinth flower to enjoy.

Waiting to Grow

Eggs, seeds, and tubers (such as potatoes) wait in the sand or dirt until the weather is right for them to start to grow. The waiting phase is called "dormant."

Potatoes grow to their full size and then lie dormant underground until spring, when a new potato plant starts to grow.

Some mosquitos lay their eggs in mud. The larvae will not hatch until it rains and the mud becomes a pool for them to swim in.

Flower seeds can lie dormant in desert sands for a long time. They only grow when the rain comes.

Glossary

Aestivation

In the summer, when there is very little water, some animals go into a long sleep. This summer sleep is called "aestivation."

Learn more about aestivation on pages 26-27.

Bulbs

A bulb is the special underground part of certain plants. The plant stores its food in the bulb and new shoots grow from there.

Learn more about bulbs on pages 28-29.

Chlorophyll

Chlorophyll is the green color in plants. Plants use chlorophyll to make food from sunlight.

Learn more about chlorophyll on pages 22-23.

Collection

You can make a collection of all kinds of things that interest you, such as stamps, shells, or autographs. For a nature collection, you must only collect things you find on the ground – don't pick flowers or leaves from growing plants.

Find out how to make a mini-museum with a collection of things on pages 18-19

Countryside

The countryside is the fields, woods, and hills away from towns and cities. It is a good place to find wild plants and animals.

Learn how to make a nature diary in the city or countryside on pages 6-7.

Dormant

When things are dormant, they are alive but have stopped growing. They wait until the weather is right for them to grow again.

Learn more about dormant eggs, tubers, and seeds on pages 28-29.

Evergreen trees

Evergreen trees keep their leaves all year round. Their leaves can be tough and shiny, or like thin needles.

Learn more about the leaves you can find in winter on pages 22-23

Herbs

Herbs are plants that have a strong smell and taste in their stems and leaves. We use herbs for cooking, making herbal teas, and even for treating illnesses.

See how you can grow your own window box herb garden on pages 10-11.

Hibernation

In the winter, when there is little food available, some animals save energy by going into a long sleep called "hibernation."

Find out how to make a winter shelter for hibernating animals on pages 26-27.

Migration

Migration is the name for the long journey that animals, birds, and insects make in order to look for food.

Find out about some amazing journeys on pages 24-25.

Thermometer

A thermometer is an instrument for measuring how hot or cold things are.

Use a thermometer for your nature diary on pages 6-7.

Index